Birdworld

Kevin Reinhardt

Birdworld

Copyright Kevin Reinhardt 2011

The right of Kevin Reinhardt to be identified as the author of this work has been asserted in accordance with the Copyright, Designs and Patents Act 1988.

ISBN: 978-0-9554989-4-7

A CIP record for this title is available from the British Library.

All rights reserved. No part of this publication may be reproduced, stored in a retrieval system, or transmitted at any time or by any means electronic, mechanical, photocopying, recording or otherwise without prior permission of the copyright holder.

Published by Vintage Poison Press.

Printed in the UK by CPI.

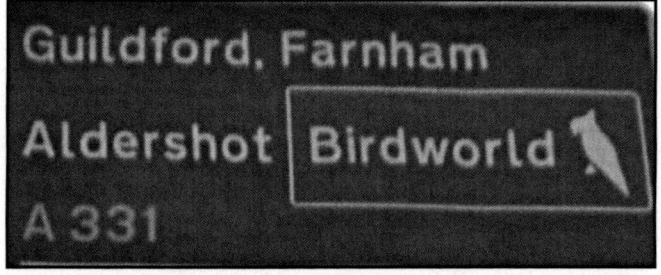

'Oh, all the poets they studied rules of verse
and those ladies, they rolled their eyes'

Sweet Jane, Velvet Underground

CREDITS AND THANKS

Thanks to the following who've in some way either directly helped with this book, booked me to read or published my poems:

Alice Bell, Hugh Metcalf, John Citizen, Jel Quinn, Robbie Chops, Jason King, Viz the Spoon, Gareth Lewis, Lucy Leagrave, Toby Davies, Joe Campbell, Paul Birtill, Jazzman John Clarke and finally the endless source of material that is my family.

Poems from Birdworld may well in some shape or form been in the following publications:

Unpublished
The Delinquent
Cake hole
words for snow
Brittle Star
Dripping

CONTENTS

BIRD

The Emperor	14
Falling in love was the best thing that ever happened to me	15
Mummy	18
Two dozen deep	20
Our star never sleeps	21
On this track, you have to get on the front foot	22
Flying V	23
Who loves the sun	24
Wedding in the family	26
Misscchhter Presscchhident	26
The amateur meteorologist	27
The Ballad of Toby Davies	27
Big John's Karaoke	27
Me and the Major	28
Masterchef	28
Demands	28
In the oversex shop we're pacting permanence	29
Fame	29
Dolly	30
Queen Sunday	30
Gunpowder to China	31
Mr Challenger bursts in pantomime through the kitchen door	32
Geoff emerges from his empire of darkness	32
Drinking guidelines for women	33
Carrie doesn't live here anymore	34
Bobby	35
Badly sung bird	36
Best poem in foreign language	36
Robert Yates Week	37
So I'm sitting in the aviary of this	38
Armchair Dancer	39
Yeah but I won the duel of kisses	40
You will dream, but you will never sleep	41

When I spoke to God	42
TV Movie	43
The day Mum killed yet another uncle	44
Rufus	45
10 reasons why Bob Dylan hates you	46
The day Bob Dylan's mother stopped taking him to the barbers	47
Cat Poem	48
So you want to know how my nan gave me a black eye?	49
Sesame Street	50
Silvia space	51
since the first time	52

WORLD

San Francisco bus ride	56
Gregory Corso is going bald (again)	57
Too extreme for California?	59
Castro	60
I know	61
Columbo in Paris	62
Dog on wheels	63
Jonathon goes country	65
Ireland, land of surprise	66
The National Institute of Pop, Amsterdam	67
Heineken advert	67
Amsterdam dude	68
Leidseplein	68
All the bars over there have them	69
The Centre of Vondelpark is at a standstill	70
Swans glide	70
The Panini sticker album of the Apocalypse	71
Berlin baby	72
David Bowie	73

Going girly girl orange in Berlin	73
Kitsch ich nicht tort	74
American youth finds itself in continental Berlin	75
Holiday in Jerez	76

GOING OUT

Nobody ever really dies	78
Minus me	79
Birdie num num	80
It's a sign	81
Swift one after work	82
New Year	82
We never liked the weeknights	83
Gents	84
Dave's band	86
Brockley	87
220	88
The night London got hammered	88
Who fancies playing the nightbus game?	91
Zoom	92
Minicab club	93
A Sunday stroll along the South Bank, amongst the bohemians	94
Excerpt from "Rivers of Blood"	96

WORK, LOVELIFE, MISCELLANEOUS

Friday	100
Fast train heaven	102
What I wouldn't give for self-lacerating Cheekbones	103
Maidenhead	104
On the road	105
EUFA Champions League Final	106

England, England, England	107
How the enemies of freedom got me the day off work	108
The night was still	109
The next week	109
Highlights	110
Hands up if you haven't got a Japanese girlfriend	111
The love song of "arm's on fire" man	111
Fucking	112
Trees, they don't like Winter	112
Beautiful and damned	113
And finally...	114
Kiss life	115
Jumpin' Jack Flash	116
Stratford	117
Chain letter	119

FIFTY PENCE MORE AND I COULD HAVE GOT SOME THAT WORKED

Fifty pence more	124
It's the Rizla that's on everyone's lips	124
Almost cured of lipgloss	125
Kevin turns to his bird	130
Necking	131
Lie To Me	132
Back to Emily's	134
What's goin' on?	134
There's a young girl I keep in the cupboard for special occasions	136
Absolute zero	137
Monday morning 9:32am	140
Susans	141

Bird

The Emperor

He's a desperate boy,
he owns a lost poem,
chases buses he's missed,
blowing kisses at them,
in the hope that they'll stop
and let him on.

He's a desperate boy,
he owns a pair of shoes
that he's never worn,
cos he had the blues
when he had no shoes,
til one day on the street,
met a man with no feet.

He's a desperate boy,
he goes CD shopping
in motorway service stations,
'Hey Kev, 'This is 'Real Country',
you didn't think
I'd Let this one
pass me by, did you?'

He's a desperate boy.
He wants to sleep all day
with a hundred butterflies
in the shape of a miracle
hovering a foot above his head,
just so that you can all watch.

I suggested he do this on a Sunday.

He's a desperate boy.

Falling in love was the best thing that ever happened to me

Every day I remember
it like it was
yesterday.

Why?
Because I can.

Driving to work
one morning
cursing various
crime-related roadblocks,

oblivious to the human
tragedy underlying it,
(mainly in chalk)

when out of nowhere
along the side of
a tower block,

against a brilliant
sky blue sky,

gymnastic in the
Hackney skyline,

I saw it.

A gold star-shaped balloon!

It captured me in an instant,
with all the allure
of a pregnant woman
on the underground.

I knew then it was love.

On that moment
all that mattered
was to be up there

200 foot above Hackney and Dalston,
me and my gold star-shaped balloon.

Instinctively I knew I had to act.
I wasn't going to live with the
consequences of not doing so.

So I fixed my gaze
up, upon on my love,
not on the road ahead.

I accelerated - death
would do me the favour,
life had more often than not
had trouble with.

I never saw it again after that.

I now lie in bed all day,
every day, being kept alive
by a combination
of tubes, machines and

not forgetting
my favourite albums
by Pulp.

Borrowed by my sister,
who'd have thought
it would've taken this
to see them again.

Every day I remember
it like it was
yesterday,

Why?
Because I can.

Except now, I get to
do this for the rest of my life.

If only my parents knew
how now I am perfect,

they'd let me be
like this,
forever.

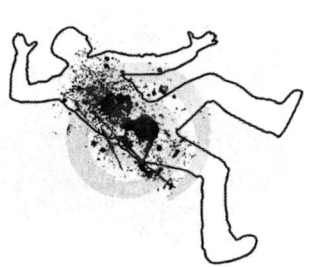

Mummy

On the top deck
of the Number 86 bus
we bask, in the early September
of my infancy

still preoccupied.

We've just been
to the butcher's
in the high street

who had a couple of top ten hits
in the mid Sixties,

pissed away his royalties
trying to keep up with
George Best

unlike his wife.

She learned to play golf
moved out to Essex
married an alchemist

who could make lipstick and cheap gold
clash all over, all over
her face.

Numerous failed attempts
at the knowledge
purely by accident

he discovered his talent for
hacking at carcasses.

Still preoccupied
by a piece of string
I hold the balloon
said butcher produced earlier
from his chest freezer.

Free to gaze, out the window,
blank, endearingly gormless,

I raise my hand
to my mouth, but for a

quick, sharp rap
across the knuckles

'Mummy'
will not tolerate
such wilful wistfulness

> *'Don't bite your nails!*
> *There might be a rapist watching;*
>
> *who'll use tweezers*
> *to handle your clippings,*
> *rest them on the breast*
> *of his next victim*
>
> *like the dejected ivory*
> *they might once*
> *well have been.*
>
> *And it won't be him*
> *they'll come looking for.'*

My hand returns
to between my legs
where it remains.

Never got to thank her
properly for that, besides

who'd want to get sentimental
over some stupid balloon.

Two dozen deep

is the crowd my Mum
swims to the front of
with absolute purpose
where she gets her
provisional driving license autographed
by neil kinnock though I am
too young to understand I feel that
things will never be the
same again and it turns out that
they aren't.

Our star never sleeps

The party that is
supermarket vodka
is over,

I'm calling a cab
for my idiot grins,

seafront flashes a smile
in need of a dentist,

this night whinges.

Pushy mum moon
nags her sky,

'Cherub, do that party piece
where you look like a duvet
for everybody here'

with no sign of sleeping,

as are you,
reaching for the
bedside drawer

wasting insomnia
with some pink thing.

On this track, you have to get on the front foot

I'm glad James Brown
is not alive.

No more not
replying to my emails,
avoiding my phone calls.

He has to talk
to me now.

So a week next
Saturday

I'm going to
ask him out
straight,

'Do you think
a Prom Queen
is vexed
with an hour of soul?'

I'll let you know what he reckons.

Flying V

Alan Hansen has stopped going
to Northern Soul all nighters,

which would explain
how I came to acquire
this green v-neck jumper.

Sporting the vest
of minor corporate celebritydom
I'm forced to drink

single malt whiskey,
as that's all I ever get bought
by people in pubs,

pose for random photos
next to BMW owners

who have opinions on
football and formula one,

practice my golf swing
when nobody's looking,

be spontaneous and witty
when everybody is, but

all I want to do is
dance dance dance dance
to the radio.

Three thousand pounds a time
for Japanese businessmen's
Karaoke nights;
it's not compensation.

Who loves the sun

A note
in the margin
of a novel
I once read

referred to it as
'options paralysis'.

Breakfast at Bridgette Bardot's
starts with the drawing
of curtains and the central heating
being turned up to full.

Her mansion houses
all the time in the world
twice over

yet seldom does she leave
the claustrophobia
of her conservatory

packed so full of
campaigns and causes
there's barely enough room
to swing a one-eyed asthmatic cat.

Today
she will rally against

those who make caesareans
of budding carnations,

church choirs who
constructively dismiss
those who sing out of time and tune,

shopkeepers who refuse
the price of a pint of milk
from the stubbled, cardiganed,
tracksuit bottomed
Mr flip-flop string vest.
.
Amidst these wrongs
she finds God,
in the microwave
of all places.

He tells her
not to get too bogged down,
to list them all out and
that it's better this way.

His sound advice is heeded,
though it's not long before
she tires of it.

That's when she marches
into the living room,
pulls back the curtains,

and at the waiting photographers
flicks them the rods.

Wedding in the Family

My sister's boss
looking round the room
observes and
points out to her

'There's only one person here
camper than your brother

and you're marrying him'.

Misscchhter Presscchhident

Abraham Lincoln's wooden teeth
were reputedly soaked in brandy;

a precedent to a little known tradition
spotted by a Texan, Johnny P Jones, who
on the eve of the 3rd of December, knowing

junior tomorrow
would be singled out by a
mildly grinning JFK

'Yes little Johnny,
what would you like to ask me?'

requested of his son that
he seek from
'Misscchhter Presscchhident'

a recommendation for a decent
bourbon to soak his dentures in.

The amateur meteorologist

catches me as he enthuses
about cloud formation.

'You should look at the sky,
you're missing out on
half the world!'

We were in the middle of a
bullshit monsoon; took
the edge off his wisdom somewhat.

The Ballard of Toby Davies

He got a slap
it was just a slap
it was a good slap
it was a good and just slap.

Big John's Karaoke

He's just seen off Elvis and
is about to take on Gene Pitney.

Leaving his half of Guinness untouched,
Roy Orbison heads for the door

as only a man in shades would.

Me and the Major
(almost a haiku)

Knife through fridgebutter
Cuts dash like a blue navy
Gold buttoned blazer
 at the oval

Masterchef

New Mum Michelle
has FAILED to identify
the yam.

'Cooking doesn't come
any tougher than this'

whistles the grand inquisitor
through insufficient teeth.

Demands

My tongue is filthy-
you can have your daughter back
in exchange for a vibrating toothbrush.

In the oversex shop we're pacting permanence

You are the fairy princess
and it has been decreed
that your ankle
is to be bitten
by the brevity of a
butterfly's purpose.

I'm the redundant cupid;
my turned bow
will scar my body.

The uspain
is very,
but shared with
nobody
but ourselves.

It is this
I think
which makes
ussmile

during what seemed
like an interlude now.

Fame

Remember my name
and the next time

you cum
you say it

nice and loud for me.
So I can hear you.
                      Wherever I am.

Dolly
(A skipping song for children)

Dolly is smart,
Dolly is pretty,
By rights Dolly should support
Chester City.

Dolly was an extra
on Hollyoaks and then

Dolly never acted, acted again.

Queen Sunday

This year,
Next year,
Sometime,
Never,
I-am-going
To work you out.

And I shall
Kill thee with much cherishing
For all the time
You fucked me about.

Gunpowder to China

Tuesday afternoon
city pub is packed by types
not worth describing,
well past their lunch hour.

Emerging from the air
thick with cigar smoke
and contempt,

he negotiates the tables
programmed like some
80s Japanese robot
working its way through a maze

from table to table
producing from a satchel
pirate DVDs which are all

Children and Hollywood
- perused and retuned – NO SALE

car chases and girls being tied up,
who come to no harm
- perused and returned – NO SALE

Chick flicks with no same-sex kissing
- perused and returned – NO SALE

He sports a pink dogtooth trilby-
his only extravagance and distraction.

Mr Challenger bursts in pantomime through the kitchen door

and with pirate abandon tosses a flat cardboard box upon the table. Flinging the lid open he reveals a lemon tart. Cutting himself a slice with the knife from between his teeth he asks,

'Do you think Steve Sumner is as well hung as John Power? They look very similar and are of a familiar stature.'

Perhaps we need some old dear to tell them apart in an ID Parade
'Yes officer, this one here. That's the baby's arm holding an orange that did the post office on the Finchley Road.'

Geoff emerges from his empire of darkness,

in a fluorescent orange tank.
He heads off to meet the

bluetoothed eared,
Bentley driving Big Mal,

landlord of the Long Good Friday up in Westferry,
who's given him the use of his lock up
ahead of the arms fair in Canning Town.

Geoff's due to rock on up there Tuesday morning.
Reckons he can get 5 grand for it.

Either way

it's gonna be a oners worth of entertainment,
or an erection.

Drinking guidelines for women

Turning to kiss my wife
goodnight

she got on there first,
tried to convince me
that she hadn't

been lashed up on booze
that afternoon and that
it was mouthwash
that had almost put me out.

I remind her of
the surgeon general's
recommendation on
women's alcohol intake,

of two thimbles a year;
one at Christmas and
of course, the Queen's birthday.

I continued by warning
my wife that exceeding
this would almost certainly

result in her rapid descent
into my uncle Eddie's divorce,

which we witnessed
as infants, when my
parents went to check on
him after Myrtle had left.

I tripped on an empty
bottle of Teachers, banged
my knee on the corner of

their coffee table and
started crying.

Eddie just sat there
rewinding and watching
the video to 'Save your Love'
by Renee and Renato.

He managed to pull through it
though, only to fall off a 30ft
scaffold, which after a lengthy
stay in hospital he recovered from

to ride his motorbike once again.
The one with the big
Pink Panther sticker
along its side.

Carrie doesn't live here anymore

She told herself
she should
love herself,

but sending herself flowers
wasn't quite what she meant.
Still,

we've all made mistakes;
who here can say that they have
never
woken up and said,

'today is great but
tomorrow's going to
be even better',

not knowing it was a
Sunday afternoon?
Hangman horoscope-
in the delirium of absence

she seemed to miss
that what was missing
wasn't him, as

she told herself
she should
love herself,

masturbating in a bed
where she slept
like a star,

a free hand feeling
a beating heart.

Bobby

'Fake Plastic Trees'
sing Santa'd up buskers;
we write in letters
to stop our thoughts being read.

It paints my eyes and lips fancy.
A received word that
all day,
you haven't had a cigarette.

Which is exactly why I called you,
to blow smoke down your voicemail.

Badly sung bird

From yellow pages
hung shirts of
the week before me

queuing up behind
the half drawn curtain
over the weekend.

Beneath the bed
your mermaid bra
swims freely amongst
the socks and
assorted underwear

just out of reach
of the dark satchel.

Best poem in a foreign language
(a poem directed by Robert Yates at The Foundry)

As commissioned by direction,
two out of every five
electro duos

have taken vaudeville,
in an attempt to reinvent.

It's enough to make
dreadlocks scream
(and they do).

It would drive you
to the refuge of corners

but for the
obdurate, inanimate
underestimated.

Robert Yates week

It's Robert Yates week!
Everybody get dressed up in black.

It's Robert Yates week!
That time of year when there's no turning back
from that
existential crisis you've been
trying to avoid.

'Come up from under the duvet
of one night stands,
sheer folly is such a ploy.'

It's Robert Yates week!
That chore that is
looking deep within your soul
and coming up with answers
to questions you'll never know.

It's Robert Yates week!
Get that last train back
home to Pimlico sober.
'Cos you don't have to be drunk
to row with
Baudelaire and Rimbaud.

It's Robert Yates week!
Translate your favourite
Smiths songs into Latin

'I wear black on the outside....'

'Cos I'm R-R-R-R-OBERT YATES!

So I'm sitting in the aviary of this

overpriced botanical garden,
blue plastic carrier bag
full of hard black liquorice
for my girlfriend,
when from somewhere I suppose
my shoulder flutters
a pigeon of ill omen-
my friend Robert,
asking me if I want to know
about his impending hospital spell.
He's parrot matter-of-fact-
the endless inspections
'one goes here,
one goes there'
south of his
Lady Godiva's circumcision.
I put the finger up his arse gag
back in the padlocked
midnight fridge, return to my bed,
my diet.
Distracted, Robert struts
towards breadcrumbs of derision,
reducing my liquorice
to no more than the bamboo toffee
of a sexless panda enclosure.

Armchair dancer

Armchair dancer,
you've got no answer to
'don't you ever sit still?'
and 'How do you go to the toilet?'

Armchair dancer,
cousin's an
unlicensed backseat driver,
jabbering on about irony
not being wasted
in their family.

Armchair dancer,
rhythm is a cancer,
paralysed from the waist down
but otherwise
a porn star.

Armchair dancer,
the light's asunder,
with the primary coloured
epilepsy
of your wedding reception uncle.

Yeah but I won the duel of kisses

no no no no no.
You beat me

at some 80s Atari pixelated simulation.

Now go get your second
and prepare for your next dawn.

You will dream, but you will never sleep

They called her Princess.
She is.

Awoken from the slumber
of one hundred lunch hours,
by a car crash.
She was.

'That's beautiful',
you tell Mamma Cass
as you ask her to turn

the light off
on the way out.

She tucks you in.
Not only are 'the good times coming,'
she adds 'they'll be coming real soon',

yet this duvet is heavy
with the guilt

of that photograph
you just couldn't take,

yet somehow managed
to steal.

When God spoke to me

It was via the usual channel;
a visitation
from The Four Tops.

With a proclamation in thunder
that took out
my parents'
living room windows

they declared that

'It was gonna be alright
I had finally got the girl'
and

though it didn't kill me
I swear I was frozen
motionless in the pose

sat at the consolation
kitchen table

when she told me it had all been a mistake.

When I eventually
got it together
to venture out the house,
I was confronted on the doorstep

with a carol singing
Public-Enemy.

TV movie

The post-chemo brain tumour woman
with between six and eight months

left to live
asks

'must you always be drunk
to think poetic thoughts of me?'

He picks a dandelion,
his kiss sending
all seeds to the wind

leaving it bald.
It's a faux pas
she manages to laugh off.

The day Mum killed yet another uncle

Dad was still nowhere to be seen,
though that may have been due to him
being eaten by a DIY store,
in a bedtime story read to me.

Breakfast was as late as school,
but it was summer and
that sort of thing was allowed.

My side of the kitchen table faced
the window,
the garden,
the summer.

Mum's the wall.

I lost what she said after,
'It's about your uncle Stephen....'

too busy watching
raisins in the cereal bowl
cling to bran flake rafts,
creating currents with my spoon.

I looked up momentarily;
I don't know
whether it was

cigarette smoke,
net curtains or
the ambient dust
that gives light shape

which gave Mum her halo
that spelt 'August'.

I suspected it was this
which lured passing milkfloats
away from lighthouses,
crashing into the pubs.
I rejoined her soliloquy at

"Cherub, long after
plastic ponies become a memory,
you'll understand.
You'll know when you meet him.
You'll know 'he's the one.'"

But Mummy,
        what if there is
no
one?

Rufus

Is universally acclaimed
(that's everybody)

as a one man
Greek Chorus.

Nobody knows
(nobody knows)

what one is;
but that's O.K.

cos we've got

Rufus.

10 reasons why Bob Dylan hates you

Pulling back the curtain
expecting the Wizard of Oz,
Dorothy shrieked

'No Calvinist was ever a cat;
is this what all this has been for?'

The wizard's stammered retort of
'your homework is late'

was met with a
'fuck you, I'm flying
with the monkeys tonight'.

I've seen you walk
the poodle perm
with that thing
women do with their legs

to stop men looking
at the backs of their hands
and guess what their age is.

My apathy is overpriced,
served in a rail replacement bus service

by a surly Pole, in a push-up-bra
her lollipop figure
so in vogue.

The day Bob Dylan's mum stopped taking him to the barbers

The ten year old Zimmerman
skips into Franco's with an abandon
which musters much gusto
on the part of Franco

'Meester Robert!
What would you like done to your hair today?
Robert produces from his satchel a copy of Blonde on blonde
and baas like the wavy lamb he probably was

'Thiiiissss one'

'I'm sorry', replies Franco with a protracted frown that still manages to beam,
'we ran out of them yesterday.' Scissors in hand, Franco then walks over to a cupboard. He returns with two albums.
'I can do you a two-for-one special between Travelling Wilbury's era Bob and Jeff Lynne.'

His scissors tick tock between them as if to demonstrate.

Cat Poem

So you want to know how my Nan gave me a black eye?

It was the only Tamil she knew
but enough to get her down the shops:

'There was this country ruled
by a King with Four Daughters'.

And no...
I didn't see it coming
when I asked

"So what's

'We came from a country
where it was said,
whoever next saved his life,
would marry
the unhappy Prince'?"

Sesame Street

My 94 year old grandmother
is on Sesame Street
at her feet

infant Hispanics
look up in awe.

From her mouth hangs
a six foot menthol cigarette
at least half of which
is ash.

Between drags
she teaches them
how to count

numbering all her friends
who've died in the past year.

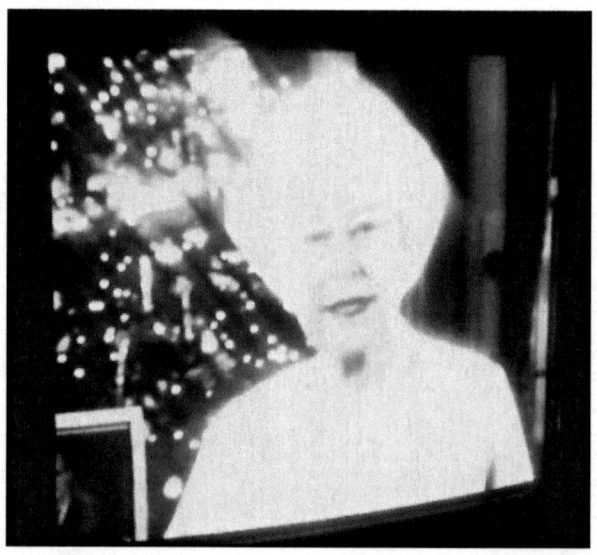

Sylvia space

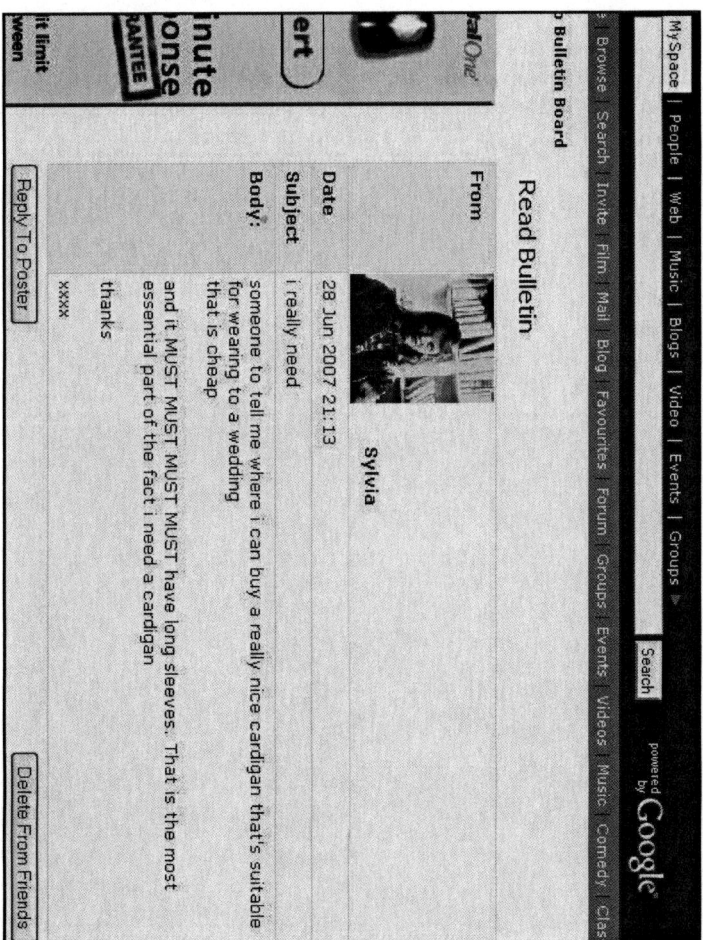

since the first time

I have given every
Wish on the
Uncertain moon to you;

I only ever needed
One, but it
Never came
True.

World

San Francisco bus ride

Cursing the driver
whose sudden stop-starts
aggravate my already fragile
hangover.

A woman of imposing frame
partly due to the numerous
layers of clothing,
boards at Market and Valencia.

On her shoulder
a Persian cat
dressed as a biker

complete with leather cap
and studded collar.

She must have been there ages
before I looked up
only to see her
staring down at me

with an ominous quiet
before the storm of

> *'Wha choo doin' in mah seat?*
> *Who said you could sit in mah seat?*
> *Choo know what I had to go through*
> *get that seat?*
> *you get on out of mah seat*
> *fore I set Billy here on you!'*

At which point
the cat shoots me
a well-timed sneer.

I get up,
make good with my apology.

The bus stops.
I alight at
Rosa Parks Boulevard.

Gregory Corso is going bald (again)

I see you, Philip T Nails, host of Amnesia, as the sightseeing bus pulls up outside of 'Rouge and Blanc' winebar. The doors opened, you jack in-the-box onto the pavement. You don't see me, through dogtooth trilby and shades, just interrupt a Gregory Corso poem I was trying to read – the one in which he goes bald-and quicker than Corso's hairline recedes, you're gone, just as I am about to say 'Hi'.

I notice the sun has gone in – no, that doesn't sound right, it's more like a shadow has been cast over me. I look up to see a bare-chested, unshaven Red Indian. He introduces himself, his spirit quite literally overwhelming me. Seated, I return the greeting, *'Pleased to meet you Elmo Red Bull. I'm Broken Bra Sniffing Dog'*.

I try not to show my impatience with Red Bull; it would be unwise for him to get the wrong idea BUT CORSO IS LOSING TUFTS BY THE SECOND! So we skip discussing how we earned our Red Indian names and I give him the two dollars he's after.

Meanwhile back in the race against time, Corso is hanging in there. Despite some very suspect imagery he's comparing his rapidly apparent lack of hair to a regression into infancy and now, being wiser of recent experience, I sense another shadow entering the proceedings.

'Hello.
Do you speak Hindi?'

'No, no Hindi, just a little German.'

*'Wie heißen Sie?
Ich heiße Ian.'*

Ian is at least 8-foot tall, about half of which is beard.
Ian also has the unique quality of making me feel like he is
the first person I have ever met whom I'd describe as
'childlike'.

'Are those Cinnamon Tic Tacs?
You guys together or just friends?
Are you my angel?'

Pulling his hair out and fuming the colour
of my glass of rosé, Corso knows the fight is lost,
cussing

The Sun which has turned on him
The girls he must now forsake
The pipe and slippers he'll be laid to rest in,

and the fact that I can tell him
what a big kid's beard looks like

or that a Red Indian with two dollars
will always return with a teddy bear

makes
not
one
bit
of
difference.

Too extreme for California?

Sunday morning, 5am,
Mardi Gras in Union Square,
the cheesecake factory working overtime.

Some dogs are big, others small;
cats, in the main, are similar in size.

All Americans have the same shaped mouth;
the philosopher within me hasn't brushed his teeth yet.

Sarah Palin claims she can hit the golden cross
off the top of Saints Peter and Paul's church,
from Coit Tower, with her rocket launcher

because it only takes the bad hair day
 of one madwoman to take down a wolf in the snow

which coincidentally, happens to be the number of members
of ZZ Top it took to shunt start, with his Monster truck,
the tram I was stuck on this morning.

Catching the business end of the mudslinging
as the seagulls of Pier 45 were deemed
'too extreme for California', I was

mistaken in thinking that,
God didn't make the little green apples and that
some Walgreens were open all night.

My midnight quest to kill the pain was thwarted,
by the laughter of a bum, speeding past in his shopping trolley,
 'Ha! Anybody who'd seen Dirty Harry
could've told you that!'

Castro

Fidel Castro has retired
relocated to the district
named in his honour,

free to roam up and down
streets steeper
than a Hitler's 'hello'

amongst the Angels and Philosophers
of some casualty or another

handing out carnations
    'had this date with inspiration,
    got stood up,
    you may as well have them.'

Who'd have guessed after Fidel's
years and years in search
of his truth

he'd find it, in a pharmacy
as Flava Flav the ballerina
pirouetted down the aisle
devouring
'Emery boards,
I need Emery boards'
called for the assistant and asked

    'Baby, why d'you have
    to lock up the soap?'

Fidel Castro has retired
relocated to the district
named in his honour.

I know

I know what you're saying,
two Mexican tourists
photographed in Jack Kerouac's alley.

Only when they see the photos
will they notice the passed-out drunk
they are in front of.

I know what you're thinking,
We're outside the San Francisco aquarium
so I take the lifesize cast of a shark's bite,

Hula hoop with it.
Anything to avoid the subject.

I know where you're coming from
now that I know which way to
look-the right way-

as opposed to where my attention was
when that bus slapped me.

Columbo in Paris

The café outside
the hotel I stay in
is slap bang in the bullseye
of red-light district Pigalle.

Sitting here, idly noting
a cartoon train with tourists and
the flailing camp flourishes

of the arms
on the windmill
of the Moulin Rouge,

little dogs outnumber the beggars
but not mopeds and certainly not
guitar shops.

Columbo comes to my table
with my coffee and croissant,
whereupon

the NEON FINGER OF TOURISM
appears above my head.
It's all in the smile
I later learn.

Mercilessly exploiting
my less than proficient
use of his native tongue

he engages me in a dialogue
regarding how you're meant
to hold a cigarette,

designed to corner me
into some crime or another.

Rather than
a bright light
in the face
to illicit confession,

Columbo decides upon
an intense Parisian
mid-morning sun,

which chooses to set fire
to the crotch of my jeans.

Dog on wheels

If cats had money
they'd make me an offer
on my gekko shoes
with high voltage
shoelaces you never tie.

As it is I've just had breakfast.
Upon my exit from the cafe
my attention arrested
by a dog

lying down flat
in a trolley
the size of a cat litter tray,

Starsky and Hutch red,
white stripe substituted
by the moniker
'Radio Flyer'.

My tourist hands
itch to snap this scene,
only to have

a voice from behind
point out
'The dog's got arthritis'.

The guilt would hang,
if it wasn't for the Columbo
'Just one thing', that being

the inverted commas
around the barely visible
tennis ball, tucked in
the dog's blanket

which apparently
it likes to chew on.

Jonathan goes country

Sleep deprivation
has finally bought about
our end.

My girl has left me
my dog hasn't got shoes to go with its outfit
this beer is flat and warm
the bar staff refuse to make eye contact
the band refuses to stop doing Neil Young covers
the insect bite on the inside of my leg is deafening
my pockets are full of people I should've said 'NO' to
this city is mine, but I don't want the responsibility.

Where are the fire engines that sound like toys?
What about that cat, in the grocery store, staring me out?

When I return to work
there will be over 300 emails to avoid
one of them will have my name on it.

Before that though,

uncertain of the sleep to come,
knowing; the indefinite hours ahead
will be spent looking for it,

do you know like a hurricane?

Ireland, land of surprises

Totalitarian in its rolling greenery
 is the twenty five minute train journey from Dublin.

Dalkey is not
without its charms, I guess,
or persistent rain.

Mists closing in on us
the nearer the top we reach,
never have I come this close
to being Paul McCartney.

Hansel and Gretelling
up a long and winding road
air mushroom-cup-a-soup thick

'Could this next blind corner
be the one
of our B-Movie-curdling screams?'

Fifty thousand pipers, emerging from nowhere,
devouring us in waves of Mull of Kintyre.

I am convinced I have pissed myself
miles from relief
where Good Friday has added
another day to the wilderness,

all hopes of getting a drink round here
flittering away with the robin
heading to a Northern soul all nighter

sporting a tank top
knitted by Julie Andrews.

The National Institute of Pop, Amsterdam

Conspicuous by their absence half hour in, it occurs to me
Take That aren't Dutch.

Had they have been,
they'd have been subsidised by the government.

'Here's your receipts for the pecs and Baby oil.'

What is it about the mentally ill
that makes them sexy?

Heineken advert

Accordion asylum seeker
is holding a pigeon.
With Meatloaf precision

he casts it into
the sky above the square.

Turning round he straps up.

Trumpet asylum seeker
points the theme to 'The
Godfather',
at the passing trams.

Amsterdam Dude

strawberry face
curly hair
blonde beard
candy striped Blazer
dirty white cravat
crumpled Khaki Chinos
permanently half filled glass of white

black eye.

The Saturday afternoon Dutch Dandy
holds court, the old and easily amused,
such as myself,
captivated
until

he is undermined
by his familiar,

a terra cotta ginger tom
breakdancing around
knotted, freestyling
elastic.

Leidseplein

In a café across the square
I spot Graham Buchan.
There's slagroom all over his tart.
He tips me the wink.

All the bars over there have them

Elizabeth Taylor
sitting outside the toilets

charging you 40 cents
to use them.

On the way out,
she gives you a lollipop.

The Centre of Vondelpark is at a standstill

There's a paralysis
of several yellow bicycles.

It's the Spaniards.

There's surprisingly little
gesticulation, given the
raised voices
and bell-ringing.

Swans glide

Through the red light district,
yet now struggle
with the composure

of every fallen stag
do in Amsterdam.

Something is up,
it's in the air.

Put your dollface on,
get your accordion out
and I'll accompany you
with mine,

to beyond
where arms flapped
till I am crossed eyed,
can take me.

The Panini sticker album of the apocalypse

Berlin baby

Nothing could be further
from looking up at the sky
than flying above clouds
that bounce rainbows at you.

Turning away from the window
casting an idle look round the cabin
a baby waves at me. I wave back.

This is my welcome to Berlin.
It rains on and off
for the rest of the day,

the infant of evening
dragged, kicking and screaming

like some fancy-dress Red Indian
taken from somewhere
they don't want to leave,
somewhere their friends are still.

David Bowie

I came to Berlin to reinvent myself.
Backed by a band which rained continuously
I slaughtered Britney Spears with karaoke,
the horror enough that I returned
in a red cagoule bought at C&A
and mirror shades.

Going girly girl girl orange in Berlin

Oranienburgerstraße's
giant synagogue
is enough to question

what Jews worship,
purely on architecture alone
or
what it is that needs to be
so closely guarded,
as the dusk brings with it
the parade and patrol of the

Jackbooted
barely skirted
Barbie dolled
brasses.

Kitsch ich nicht tort

Goethe lived till 83,
his more colourful compatriot
Friedrich Schiller, 46,

whose flowing mane of infinite curls
never forgotten when Germans snack
on the fried, rolled up shark fins,
Schillerlocken.

Meanwhile the Manic Street Preachers
renege on their promise of blood
to make a first and final album,
stay beautiful, be no more.

Who'd aspire to be
the German Shakespeare

when you could
immortalise your hairdo
in dead sharks.

American youth finds itself in continental Berlin

Monday night-
the US want Lemmy for President,
this bar has a VHS recorder,
we watch WarGames,
Scott Walker sings of girls and dogs,
it's all sofas and cocktails.

All fun and games
until the first rape allegation,

the playboy prince frat
currently managing
two girls on his lap,
with room for one more.

The chubby blonde's
having none of it.

Too busy
majoring in
photojournalism.

Holiday in Jerez

Breakfast is in a high ceiling
red-walled dining room.

I do not speak Spanish.
This does not matter.

I am surrounded
by the International
Conspiracy of Grandmothers.

They hardly speak.
They don't have to.

Later that day
Robbie Williams
will meet his end in a bull ring.

But for now,
over piped music,
I'm being threatened,

by Nina Simone.

Going out

No one ever really dies

Unending and ceaseless war on the nerds.
Hands slammed in doors so they write like infants.
Duffle coats ablaze, Paddington bear Buddhists.
Piss on their fires, from fuzzy felt fire engines.

Hands slammed in doors so they write like infants.
Spazzing out discord with lollipops on xylophones.
Piss on their fires, from fuzzy felt fire engines.
Toy town bladders cannot save you now.

Spazzing out discord with lollipops on xylophones.
Incinerating to Graham Coxon yelps of self delusion.
Toy town bladders cannot save you now.
Spend more on a ukulele than most would do on a
Mortgage.

Incinerating to Graham Coxon yelps of self delusion.
Two hundred quid NHS style glasses, your remains.
Spend more on a ukulele than most would do on a
Mortgage.
Unending and ceaseless war on the nerds.

Minus me

I only popped in for a pint,
avoided the stares
of the cheese and pineapple
as I fingered the eye buffet, but

by then it was too late!

Jukebox megalomania!
I had to enforce my
boy band moves

to take over the dancefloor
if not the world, and then

she walks into my fist,
me! Apache dancing,
invoking the skies
to deluge Morrissey,

through which concussion
she spoke to me and said,

'You do realise I'm total Lesbian
- minus you',

as my Elvis impersonation
left the building, taking with it
my shyness, which it was
carrying like a sicknote.

Birdie num num

There's a load of pig-whipping going down in St Albans
and the word is a piercing known as 'The Frankenstein'
is said to be the answer to the left-sided problem.

'You can't have him all – SPIT ROAST!'

One superhero and his goalkeeping dog-
I could watch this all night
but I don't have to as I have cable

and I've got my tent with me
cos I'm not fighting for a piece of floor
even if we did so
 in slow motion.

That's not her boyfriend,
Look!
Body language, ill-fitting jacket, only been worn once.

All this as a tartan-turbaned empress is writing a poem
that will kill the sun

sweetened
with lipstick and Coca-Cola,
dancing
like it's a Mad, Mad, Mad, Mad World.

It's a sign

It's unusually quiet
for a saturday night

a rare chance
to take in the scenery
at the urinal.

but it's not
the space
and time
on my washed hands
that stares into
the back of my neck.

it's a condom machine.

a sign.

opportunity
back pocket bulge
serendipity
nugget, nugget.

a sign.

slot, knob, coin.
aim, fire, turn.

halfway there.
definitely a sign.

slot, knob, coin.
aim, fire, turn.

it's a sign
that says
'Please insert both coins before turning knob.'

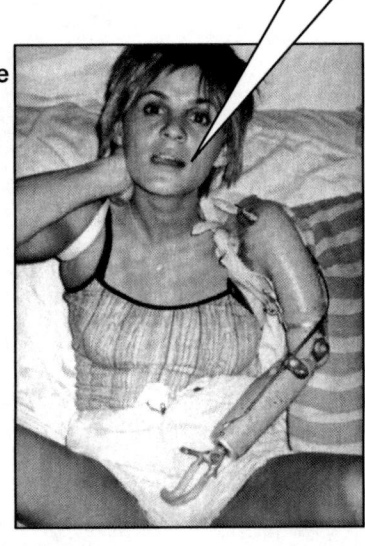

Swift one after work

In station pub 'The Islamabad'
far too much faux mirth is being drunk

during the split second I shut my eyes tight
that Donkey is braying at its own jokes
as whatever it's raping
shrieks Estuary Dalek.

I sell my eyewitness account
to the tabloids

it's enough
for another round of drinks.

Smoking is bought back
 in pubs,
which is fortunate,
not just for me.

New Year

Balloon suicide is rife.
They'd rather take
their own helium

than be raped by
revellers.

I,
said the sparrow,
I murdered disco.

We never liked the weeknights

You're either boring
or repressed.
I need the sleep.

As the evening ends
you urinate
nowhere near as straight

as a sundial
cast in moonlight.

From the neck up,
I'm a precarious vase,
filled and tottering
with alcohol and ambition.

Gents

'An ostrich with its head in the sand
ignorant to vibrating trousers
will soon acknowledge
seeping desperation'
– Old South African proverb

'Anglo Saxons and their drink'
a Latin acquaintance observed
one Saturday evening.

Halls this big used to hold
table tennis tournaments,

now they ignite whatever
optimism-fuelled carnage
lies the wrong side Sunday.

Collared by my bladder
my desperation soars

The ladies are at hand
(typical)
The gents are upstairs
(typical)

step, step, step, step, step, step, step, step
confuse concentration for distraction

till at the top
thinking of relief
which sounds too much like release

I lead the charge
one hand
belt fly zip cocked

the other
jousting arm
aimed at the door

only to be unceremoniously
unsaddled, floored by the
pungent wave of OZONE!

Who put a photocopier
in the gents?

Man at the urinal,
Man at the urinal,
Man at the urinal,
Man at the urinal,
Man at the urinal,
Man at the urinal,
Man at the urinal,
Man at the urinal,
Man at the urinal,

please replace the paper in tray 1.

Dave's band

Dave's band, shaking it
baby lamb, before even a note
How cute! But all they do for
internal tourism, 'it's the keys to Camden!'

Their work's cut out
with this buffet of indifference.
Lucky for them 'The Other Dave'
has shown. This bearded, earplugged
wraith of their youth
follows them round North London,
like their uncles before them.

It's a slalom to the bar,
past Quant-fiended girlalikes
muttering vacant prayers to the
Goddess of Vaguely Tolerable Boyfriends,
who deliver unto them

Adam. Drumming one hour ahead of
alpha Dave time, it's this
testosterone theatre
the skirt well and truly digs.

Such machiavellia
will not leave Dave undone,
it's his finger on the
rock and roll panic button-
'If you can't impress, CRASH'.

Fame has left her phone
at home tonight;
still, she manages
to talk Dave down
into graceless mediocrity.
As the truly young

discover their talent
for looking genuinely lost,

a Chariot of Adam charges
back beyond the stage and

I leave my T-shirt buying
for another Dave.

Exit flyering makes a
landlady of my eyelids,

No Pakis,
No Nig nogs,
No Actors,
No Irish.

No badly applied eyeliner
And definitely, no hairgrips.

Brockley

The man who put his hand on my balls
I didn't argue with, nor did I dare challenge
his infantry of 2 pence coins lined
along the edge of the pool table

so I put the next 5 pound coins to good use-
one hour forty of Dusty Springfield's greatest hits

'In Deptford,
you don't go drinking without your Fairy Godmother
or Cilla Black.'

220

Someone on this bus smells of garlic.
As I stand up to get off, out from under my coat
leaps the target sign the DSS use
to spot benefit fraudsters.

After searchlighting the top deck
it returns to me shaking from side to side
'not the kebab, not the kebab'.

The night London got hammered

Do you remember
exactly where you were
the night London got Hammered?
What do you mean no?

We went to that pub in Ilford,
The Two Ronnies, which used to be
The Nightmare on Elm Street
until "that rival sitcom shooting"
which made John Sullivan
a marked man in Essex.

My Nan had just won
Pensioner Idol.
We were out celebrating
her debut single getting to No1.

Goths had been decriminalised,
Mods downgraded to class A
so although blackcurrant
was freely available behind the bar,
you had to go round the back
to pick up a Parka.

God
was 2-1 up on the pool table
against the agnostics,
the banter a bit heated
but nothing too serious

and you lent Satan
a fiver because he forgot
the PIN Number for the fruit machine.

We entered
the pub quiz.

'Only one Department of Social Security
employee per team please.
House rules.'

Round one.
TV and Film.

Question One.
'Who do you think you are?'

We argued for ages
over the answer.

Neither of us were right.

We ended up third.
One point behind joint winners
'Dr Zhivago's Abortion Clinic'
and 'The Four Postmen of the Apocalypse.'

Last bell tolled
and after pouring out onto the pavement
like an Action Man in the invisible night

believing, perception
was nine tenths of the law

I sought hope in the mouth
of a Trojan Horse, as we caught
the last snog home.

Now do you remember?

Who fancies playing the nightbus game?

It says something, when you have to scribble your chat-up
lines all over a bungled rainbow, a single launch at a
butterfly whose Dusty Barnet is doing it for me more than
the Xeroxes of anaemic liquorice boys, troupes of cycling
tops, so loud the audience went luminously deaf.

You say 'unfortunate' but it's not me who has to put up with
blamange heaving cleavages, rugby songs sung through rose
red inbred cheeks.

So as you find me here, Christian of Nigeria; my kisses have
been misplaced as you can tell by all this pink paint over my
lips

Which, if it unsettles you like I know it must,
you should see what the word of God has done
to the state of my teeth.

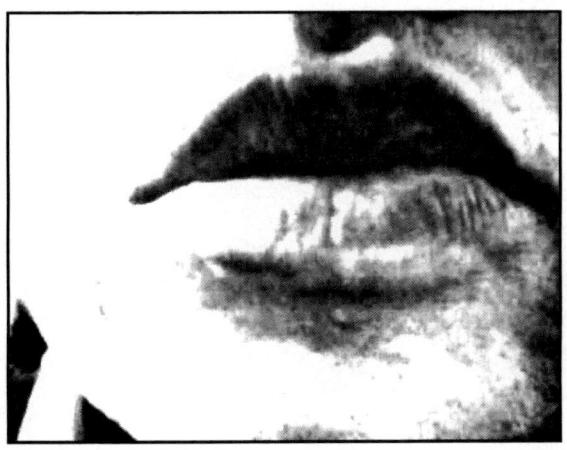

Zoom

The poxy Harrow Road-
'All day I've been traipsing up and down it!'
complains a second-hand tramp

this recalled by my often-gets-mistaken-for-one-best-mate
who had been out on his bike and bumped into
said horses mouth.

The poxy Harrow road-
yet another Red Hot Chilli Peppers insipid cover version,
Ghanaian minicab drivers obliging requests
for Heart, Magic and Fat Larry's Band.

Outside my flat
before bed
the 2am sunset cigarette

There's a fox in my bins,
starts as I light up,

behind me the arch of Wembley stadium
still lit twinkling Silver Surfer piss.

I point this out to the fox,
we share a moment.

And then
My whole wide world went -
Zoom

Minicab club

If I was a minicab driver and I picked myself up late one Sunday night, I'd have no reservations about myself because I'd be put at ease by my pleasant demeanour and general well-turned-out appearance. I'd certainly have no problem obliging myself when I asked if I could stop at the nearest cash point to get the £35 required for the fare. I suspect I'd be a little bemused watching myself return from the cash point to start tapping on the window waving two £20 notes. Curious, but by no means suspicious, I'd then roll down my window and tell myself we could sort out the fare when I got back in the car, only to have me request that I wait a few minutes as I was dying for a piss and had found a conveniently hidden alleyway. I'd be fine with that and would take the opportunity to turn the radio on, tune in to Magic FM and enjoy 'Zoom' by Fat Larry's Band for the seventh time that evening, chuckling as I rehearsed my favourite joke, the one where I tell myself as the journey has well and truly commenced, 'You can't get 5ive in a cab, but I will play Boyzone'. Much before that though, I would, however, ask when I got back in the cab whether I'd pissed all over my shoes.

A Sunday stroll along the South Bank, amongst the bohemians

I had no idea
this kind of thing
still went on.

Dad, for the purposes of visualisation,
has a jumper over his shoulders,
arms tied in a knot
which cannot be undone
over a salmon-pink-polo-shirt
all Ralph gone wrong.

Opposite,
a squatting sky-blue v-necked man
(possibly Eastern European, aren't they all)
who before him has two obligatory
one yellow, one blue
budgies – perched on a tray
while at their feet
are brightly coloured cards and for
two pounds fifty said budgies
will jump down off their perch,
hop about and choose a card for you
which when upturned reveals the gender of your next
wife or something,
well opposite him

is this ice-cream van
where Dad buys his can't-be-much-older-than-six son
a 99.
With flake.

As Dad is handed back his just-about-change-from-a-tenner
before he has a chance to exclaim
'Where's your mask?'

a where-did-that-come-from opportunistic skateboarder hits Dad square on, leaving with wallet as quickly as he appeared.

'The Boy' is hysterical with tears.

'Well go on then.
Don't just sit there bawling your eyes out.
You're the one in the Spiderman outfit, do something.
Here, I'll hold your ice cream while you go after him.

Excerpt from Enoch Powell's famous 'The notorious Rivers of lucozade' speech, as delivered in Birmingham on 20 April 1968.

All the style, leaping immigrants of Olympic enterprise.

Watch them flares check, catholic heathen to understatement

blinding Christmas with 'Fuck your Diwali'

Friday

The girl in front in the red MG
dances motorway kiss chase
as we leave the M3.

Arrive at work,
'Mother's at Sea!'
we all run riot
then stop for tea, in this

Godot-forsaken business park
in the middle of Surrey,
I chain smoke like my Nan
until I'm free, to lunch on

egg, coleslaw and houmous sandwiches
in the only canteen
that gets away with
walls
bell-Jar yellow
and carpets
abortion-clinic green.

Back upstairs
'Yeah I'll have that cup of tea'
clock holds its breath
as phones empathetically scream

'IT'S ALWAYS YOU, YOU, YOU WITH
ME, ME, ME!';
exhaling clock sighs
'Five-Thirty'.

Like a bat out of Guildford
bombing down the A3,
only to have to baggage-carousel
round the M25
(Which for the purposes of this poem goes past the M23)

Last Orders! looked like a goer
but now all the hope I see,
dances away like errant carrier bags
towards a dead balloon tree.

Finally parked up outside my flat,
pumpkins closing in on me,
there's literally seconds
left of Friday;

but unlike you Cinders,
they belong to me.

Fast train heaven

IRA HUNGER STRIKER REVIVALIST!
screams his hairdo
louder than the Human League
between my ears during the 40 minutes

I try to ignore between Maidenhead
and Paddington day in day out
and what with the scene that this makes
my gaze swings across him
like the mast of a yacht,
ready to knock him square

but he ducks, bobs back up
and is now throwing
caged wildlife shapes
at the surrounding passengers

who have resolutely
nailed eyeballs to their laps.

All this, before Slough.

What I wouldn't give for self-harming cheekbones

tea-pot poise,
depth to match.

One foreigner asks another
whether they have enough LEGO
to buy a football club.

I'm staring at the sun
in the third person,

a sensation I haven't experienced
since my acquaintance with
long-term unemployment
and television.

For the second after
I turn from the light
everything is X-ray

You ever been on a train
that flew through trees?

Could you point out where you were
on the map, before you realised
they spoke English?

Could you please re-enact
with these dolls
what exactly the big magnet
wiped out?

Maidenhead

To all intents and purposes
it's a Polish grocers
fronted by a Chinaman

with only one 'no questions asked'
facial expression
I've grown accustomed to

even over the most legitimate
of transactions, which this happens to be-
ten Marlboro menthols.

Except tonight, late, Tuesday
where home seems further than usual
something's different.

Of course, It's not him
but I check all the same.

It's the till-
on the front is a sign
courtesy of Thames Valley Police

warnings of on-the-spot fines
if found in possession
of minor-bound booze.

Behind me, a man
whose aura and appearance
at worst stirs suspicion,
at best
begs speculation.

None of which is helped
as I leave and catch his
claims of 'It's not for me - really!'

It's not so much that we
shoot ourselves in the foot
it's that we take aim first.

On the road

Her business done for today,
now unpacked in a suitably dirty
weekend B&B

a Thomas Hardy landscape
and the football highlights
vying for her attention.

For yet another not quite
post-coital cigarette,
she parts the pleated-skirt curtains;
window opens, as far as an arm.

Off the balcony
the butt is tossed,
she sings to the pavement
'Fly, fly, fly, fly.....fly
my dove'.

Flick fancying the remote
Channel 4 corners her
with a woman she won't.

An aspiring minor celebrity
interior decorator,
pert, lollipop pout
delivering civil service diction,

whose general condescension,
sashaying and patronising
brings about the transfiguration

of a lower league (probably Northern)
aspirational mid-terrace
as tearfully delirious homeowners

show their gratitude
with an impromptu
celebratory mambo.

This chill in the June evening air
will herald her sexless summer of

Motorway Service stations,
prosaic erections.

UEFA Champions League Final

21 May 2008 – Luzhniki Stadium – Moscow
Manchester United 1-1 Chelsea (Manchester United win 6-5 on penalties)

As the Chelsea players go up to collect their reward for being broken, the despondency that saturates them suffocates all thoughts of the inevitable bullet to the back of their head, the black bin-linered sleep in some Moscow suburb which their rest will be marked by.

Player by player dolefully files past till all that is left is Avram Grant.
After being anointed in defeat, Sepp Blatter pulls him close for a final word of consolation.

Sepp: I'm sorry.
Avram: Thank you.
Sepp: I mean, about the result.
Avram: I know, thank you.
Sepp: Good, good

England, England, England

The true price of austerity,
no sixteen piece orchestra
for popular T.V. theme tunes

and now Maida Vale
looks more like East Berlin
than East Berlin does.

Take That sing at men
with handbag sized dogs.

Who's ever had flowers
for breakfast?
Exactly,

me neither, so
why is the florist
round here open so early?

The albino in the mosque we pass,
inside the bus, reflected
in the window, the faces

of everyone I won't
make eye contact with
on the way to work and

a million love songs later
I still can't deal with
being 'a bit too cute'
for Alan Shearer.

How the enemies of freedom got me the day off work

The enemies of freedom
got me the day off work,
bob-a-job boy scouts
buffing their dirty bombs.

I'm out, towards the shops
it's cold, I can hear

my hat admit consequence
as I look for someone
to keep my ears warm.

Fate's not real,
luck, though, is
and mine's just changed

two maverick sisters;
Siamese.

Of no use
despite limbs
in all the right places.

Cold eared
lost purpose

I return to my plague pit
and prepare for government.

The night was still

Not two-week-old-bottle-of-Coca-Cola still
but the silence after we asked
one hundred minicab drivers
to name five straight matinee idols.

All that stirred was the hair
on the back of my neck;
the breath of my mid-life crisis
so close, I turned and whispered

in its ear

'that mediocrity my youth
so lusted after,
you're welcome to it.'
That,

the dartboard
the pornography
and the air rifle.

Next week

AIDS
is about the same age
as Hip Hop...

next week
on the History of the Twentieth Century

The Stone Roses debut album
and how it sounds better now
than it did back then

but not much.

Highlights

She sits me down on a chair
in the middle of my kitchen
puts her bag down and unzips.

An apron round my neck,
fingers through my hair,
'What you after?' she asks.

'Troubled, Australian soap teenager neon orange, '
I tell her 'and not Maroon Male Model
voted off Big Brother in Week 3'

I don't need random Shouts of 'FAGGOT'
from postmen on the way to work.

She only has Midnight Blue.
Later in the bathroom mirror,

I stumble upon a mid-life crisis
I wasn't looking for.

It's the raven haired pensioner
with her 20-year-old boyfriend
off that documentary-

Jason, that gay bloke
with the receding hairline
my sister worked with,

used a permanent marker pen
to fill in
the bits that weren't hair.

Hands up if you haven't got a Japanese girlfriend

You just about feel spring, like
valentines hitting the doormat
and all that.
Those birds are out again;

it's raining lighters
as they return
what they've hoarded over winter.

For a moment,
you're light,
pushing round regret
in a supermarket trolley

full of lard.
The air is
twice your lungs.

The love song of 'my arm's on fire' man

This isn't love,
this is this;

long though it burns,
the less hang I get of it.

Fucking

Up the chance to die young,
suffering the pain of a man
who doesn't write his own gags,

punctuating it all with
cameo sex.

Looking:
to be blinded by a sun
or even a sign of one,
behind a sky where something like a
yes
no
love
hangs.

It is then
and usually
around this time, that

lighting strikes twice,
in a bed half its size.

Trees, they don't like Winter.

Every autumn,
every morning as I would go to school,
every tree that I would pass
would wave out to me
with a million little
copper mittens.
Within weeks
they would be
flicking me the rods.
That's when I realised that
trees
they don't like winter.

Beautiful and damned

Today,
procrastination isn't
as procrastination doesn't.

I must put a stop
to what I am in danger
of getting round to.

It exhausts me;
leaping from my balcony
swinging from my chandelier

swashbuckling my phantoms
all of them
all at once.

Long after the cameras
have packed up and gone

Stevie Wonder's still singing
'Heaven help us all.'

And finally...

History repeats itself
first as tragedy
second as farce

Marilyn Manson covers
Depeche Mode, Personal Jesus.

A knowledge of literature
that doesn't get past adverts
shows technique, without credential.

I should really
thank her, but
there's doubt
I'll get round to it.

My parents throw
in hope, one eyed cats
at TV evangelists

The hangover of Dorian Gray
was compounded
when he woke one Sunday,
saw Dagenham
looking better than he did.

We're getting
the band back together,
we should do lunch
sometime soon

that is as parallel
as lives that never meet get

Kiss life

*This kiss life sucks itself
ninety nine percent!*
jumped the thoughts of these typewriters
from the top of this merchant bank.

Unimpressed, as they were engrossed by
an elderly Sikh turbaned
lollipop man,
the first brunette
to stop traffic in these parts.

Upon impact bounced ideas
set off in pursuit
of a man-sized chicken for the
next twenty six miles.

Chase exhausted,
wrapped in margarine-sponsored foil
they discovered plastic tea
was no good for the soul, ahead of

but overshadowed by
the prize-winning news
that such evidence was found
in fossilised robots

commencing speculation
of how we came to be
who we are,

just as there will be nights,
when there's where we'll end

on the back of a matchbox,
a cornflakes packet,
or maybe even
the answer to a pub quiz question.

Jumpin' Jack Flash

Not being a morning person,
it being Mother's day tomorrow
causes
Saturday afternoon shopper claustrophobia

Oxford Circus sends my sciatica spastic, penalty
for not being Organised Son Number One.

Unimpressed by advances in fair-trade face-care products
I am just about ready to slash my wrists in Body Shop
with a foot loofer, which a security guard snatches from me
in time. They're out of White Musk.

He sends me across to the till,
demands I purchase the second-best efforts
which feels a magnitude more than inadequate;
his playground laughter confirms this.

Within a jumpin' jack flash
the gale outside
makes atrocity of bad hair days,

Centrepoint may as well be Godzilla
hurtling cycle couriers, taxis and jaywalkers
into a the back of a skip
(to mass encouragement).

A traffic warden, before they get the chance
to put pen to ticket, is tossed several stories up
like a grape trying to be caught in a mouth-
fortunate as we were about to be double yellowed.

'Have I forgotten where we parked?
 I can't find our car'
I turn to ask you.

Too late, you're gone.

Stratford

I finished my first book recently,
had absolutely no idea what it was about, but
I figured all experience was good
so being more stupid after reading a book
was something I could tick off the list
although I wish it had been a longer book,
because I've just seen what's next,

and it's crocodile arm wrestling.

Like you once said
it's not a play about depression
it's not a play about relationships
it's a play about trust.

TRUST! WHAT DO YOU KNOW ABOUT TRUST!

The last person I lent my library card to
is now wanted in three postcodes and
is now known to the local police as
Kid Orange, though if you're interested I'll be outside

the Exchange in Ilford like I am most Saturday mornings,
bulk buying five lighters for a quid.
We were going to take this to Edinburgh
until I was with tested positive with an allergy to minority
interest TV and diagnosed BBC2 intolerant, like my Aunt
who bought my Dad and I matching sweaters for Christmas.
I threw mine back in her face, stormed out screaming

IT'S BAD ENOUGH BEING HER SON!

Well that's all well and good Mr Reinhardt but all I asked you
was 'have you done any work-paid or unpaid-in the last two
weeks?'

But that's not why I'm here to talk to you tonight.

I'm here to talk to you about God.
Do you think about God?
God thinks about you.
He's been thinking about you a lot recently.

God
has asked me to come here tonight

AND PLEAD WITH YOU not to go to the newspapers.
Look I know what he did was stupid but you were both drunk
and it was a Christmas party for Christsakes! His career
could be in ruins over this and for what? A packet of
chocolate biscuits and a signed photo of Max Clifford?

All I'm asking you to do is sleep on it,
Sorry what was that again?
Look, before I go to the bar I need to pop over to the
newsagents,
I've lost my lighter even though I've got loads at home,
HOW ANNOYING IS THAT?

Stratford, this is Stratford.
The train calling at Platform 8
will call at Maryland and Forest Gate.

Stratford, this is Stratford.

Chain letter

Walk like you're breaking in a pair of new shoes.
Cuss like that mongoose who gave you a black eye.
Relax like a milked cow.

Drink like you've been dumped
by someone you weren't going out with.
Smoke like some 94 year old's grudge with God.
Floss like a bank manager with nothing else to do.

Sing Karaoke like it was a good idea at the time.
Speak to tourists like they owe you money.
Comb knots like a good boy scout.

Explain yourself to policemen like they were pensioners.
Prepare a meal like it was your prisoner's last.
Search for issue 177 of 'Jackie' like it was on the run.

Stalk like you don't need the autograph.
Turn on a friend like an umbrella in a gale.
Buy a watch for somebody like James Bond.

Give it 'the big I am' like a bulletproof monk.
Put your hands in someone's pockets when told to
'stop folding your arms'.
Fill a shoe like a man with indigestion.

Graduate like a cross-dressing TV evangelist.
Enthuse like a social worker who's just been
backpacking round Thailand.
Find friendship like a comfortable pause.

Be as still as one of the many ceramic dogs
on your Nan's mantelpiece.
Outstare cats when poker is eventually made illegal.
If you want to stop being bored, you can start by taking your
hand out of that glove puppet.

Remark on the ugliness of a baby
like you knew what was coming next.
Sleep like you didn't know tomorrow would be your last.
Paint a rainbow with felt pens and photocopies, for the sake of tourism.

If you've been paid what you were owed, ask directions from a policeman like they were the tourists.
Work like a farmer choreographing a dance routine
for a talking pig.
Electric boogaloo that fish out of water.

Laugh like somebody else is telling your joke.
Look at tattoos of Brian Sewell like they were that exchange student your parents favoured over you.
Say it like you meant it to sound like the weather forecast.

Rock like the candy on Southend sea front.
Run through the videogame dark alleys your life is on Saturday nights.
Cry me a river the Silver Surfer would get out of bed for.

Judge others like you'd like to be judged on Masterchef.
Treat elephants like camels and camels like sharks.
Play it again Mario, arrivederci Popeye.
Hope like you got the party hat in the Christmas cracker.
Chase small animals around your flat like a caveman.
Fill a glass of water like it was a glass of water.

Tolerate unwelcome guests like those chimpanzees you've always wanted to slap, but couldn't.
Give your mates a lift to the pub like you were on Double Bubble.
Drink absinthe like you were listening to AOR,
on state-of-the-art German headphones.

Wish on a Kinder Surprise like it was a falling star.
Run for a bus like democracy depended on it.
Find a guy, like a guy finds you.

Change your mind quicker than a Chinese table tennis
Olympiad, so you can keep up with women.
Turn back time like you were Christopher Reeve.
Scream like a girl every time you manage to beat Alex
Ferguson at Pool and he has to buy the drinks.

Point at children like they could drum like Dennis Wilson.
Point at Charles Manson like he could surf like Brian Wilson.
Treasure soap like you'd befriend a loner.

Gather dust in a Library like antiquated socialism.
Devour horoscopes like ostensibly well-meaning aimless
liberals.
Disguise the contempt of an Etonian with an 'I suck lemon'
smile.

Fifty pence more and I could've got one that worked

Fifty pence more and I could've got some that worked
(The screenplay to a life never to be filmed)

Opening scene:
Kevin is staring in the bathroom mirror.
The bright sunlight that illuminates him should suggest it is late morning. He is relaxed but looks deep in thought, not sure what he should be checking for or out.

It is important to note, he is unaware that this will be the only moment he has to himself
in the next year and a half.

Bending down towards the sink, Kevin's reflection temporarily disappears.
It re-emerges brushing it's teeth.......
(to be read as Kevin brushes his teeth)

It's the Rizla on everybody's lips

the bus I almost kiss
at the centre of
girl adventure
stamp
on the tip of my tongue
- philately

(rinse, gargle, then spit)

Yes, you heard.

Kevin is never left alone. Not even in his sleep.
They've just bought back Pop Quiz to Channel 5 and it's being hosted by my parish priest, who I haven't seen in years. On my team is Miss Peru, who went on to win Miss World that year and then take over the Radio 1 Breakfast show.
As soon as Father O'Connor asks in the quickfire round 'Name somebody with a good ear for music', I buzz in
BUZZZ!
'MARK E SMITH, LEAD SINGER WITH THE FALL'
Miss Peru turns to me and laughs,
'Good answer'
except the other team now starts buzzing in
BUZZ, BUZZ, BUZZ, BUZZ

It's Kevin's Alarm.
He springs upright.
It's 11:15 AM.
It's Saturday.
Sighing, he slumps back into bed and almost instantaneously jolts back up.
He can't remember what it is he's late for, but he's late.

On the back of his hand it reads......

Almost cured of lipgloss

Waking not knowing
the day or the name
you find yourself under

the dictionary definition for worse, but
there's not time to see
if there are any clues in

the bathroom mirror
as to what you should be
checking for or out, as

there are daydreams in Soho to be had.
Fortunately there is lost time to credit by
a catlike quickened pace
along that stretch of road to the station
where someone you look like
got stabbed.

This bit on the platform
is critical. You have to
suppress the urge
to tell the accordion player
she is shamelessly

lifting lyrics from
Cocteau Twins
album tracks.

There's a newspaper
with your name on it
and yet another
who looks like you.

More snakes, not enough ladders
as at your destination
you piss precious minutes -
you've boarded the wrong
end of the train
'schoolboy, schoolboy' and
for all that it matters
you may as well be wearing
boxing gloves
with your shoelaces undone.

Pity rains on you.
You've missed the state opening of
the pie and mash shop
on Tottenham Court Road by
some dancing pearly King of a Monkey
with a face you can't get rid of
and a name you'd rather not place,
but It's OK Really
because by way of consolation
you manage to catch
the Royal National Institute for the Blind's
annual abseil down the side of Centrepoint, except

exasperation tugs vigorously at your arm
compels your attention
to something your parents once told you about
across the street

- 'That's not what a real transvestite's
meant to look like!' So

you go on over.
Amidst remonstration,
cat fur and the odd
false flying nail

with an arm now free of indignation
you produce from up your sleeve
'A SUPERMAN'

emerging from a phone box as
'NATALIE WOOD!'
'MAMMA! I AM A STAR!!!'

The window shattering shrill
that gives chase to that charlatan
ducking and diving
every Ann Summers and La Senza.

DUSTY

loving will not make you a bad man

It's Saturday evening, Kevin is in his local with his bird (who is a performance poet) and his friend Geoff. They're celebrating; Geoff's Divorce has finally come through from his wife who is missing, presumed dead.

The pub is fairly quiet and the only character of note is a svelte tandoori-chicken-tan middle-aged man at the bar. He keeps asking Geoff if he wants to play with his little dog 'Oscar', the leashed Scotch Terrier at his side.

Kevin turns to his bird

Kevin: Go on then, give us your new poem.
Bird: Tweet, tweet.
Kevin: It's a Haiku.
Bird: tweet, tweet.
Kevin: Well let's hear it then.

Bird: tweet, tweet, tweet, tweet, tweet.
Kevin: View from Balcony.
Bird: tweet, tweet, tweet, tweet, tweet, tweet, tweet.
Kevin: Cabbage patch of cleavages.
Bird: tweet, tweet, tweet, tweet, tweet.
Kevin: God winks at my farm. That's disgusting.

Kevin looks unsettled by this. Geoff informs him that this is not outside the norm and in fact
birds doing filthy poems tend to go do well at poetry events. Apparently it's all the rage.

At this point Geoff's mobile phone goes off.
Kevin and his bird look at Geoff expectantly...

Necking

Yet another
all talk, no teeth
text message
on my mobile

from Barbara Streisand.
Says she's going to
exact revenge

on my pretty, pretty
neck.

Turns out there's
been a misunderstanding.

It was from
long time collaborator
The Bee Gees'
Barry Gibb.

A man whose gnashers
surely warrant retribution.

And hair.
let's not forget the hair.

This looks like being the highlight of their evening, but then, they've no idea what's about to come through the pub doors.

DON'T YOU FORGET IT

BOYO BONO & YOKO

Lie to Me

The Landlord of
the Barrel of Monkey Laughs
and Firkin,
in an attempt to obtain
a cheque the size of a road sign,

is polishing the inside
of a pintpot
with a rag which, to all intents
and purposes, might as well
be emery paper.

As he heads towards
the anecdote cabinet
to get out that time

a poodle dressed as Cliff Richard
was found throwing up
drunk in the toilets
during the pet version
of stars in their eyes

I flounce in, hijack
the most banal of silverware

'Oi Oi!
LOOK WHO IT IS EVERYONE!
IT'S LIZ – THE PONCE!'

In my Afghan coat
I slalom to the bar,
lighting up and dragging
on liquorice

should all of a sudden
I get struck down
with French Cinema

They are willing captives
to my stories of
faraway exotic Berkshire.

'It's OK. I'll have
my peppermint tea
without the strainer.

That's how they drink it in Slough!

And d'you know those
mobile phones you got,
I've got photos
of the buildings that control them.

Bigger than a premiership
football manager,
visible from continental Europe.'

You lot are sooooo last Tuesday!

Sauntering over to the Jukebox
coquettishly flicking
my fringe, I say
'Haven't you got any Jack Johnson?
That's what they're all listening to in Marlow'

'OH LIZ!'
They gasp
'YOU'RE SUCH A PONCE!'

A Ford Fiesta pulls up
as my exit flourishes to the door.

Before I skip off into the back of it
I spin round on my heel,
twisting envy into their backs,

'Me and some cats
are off to a Heston Services
Ginster pasty all-nighter
Yeah.'

Back at Emily's

After a night of overpriced tango and dancing to various compilation albums (including,
'Now that's what I call a Ford Mondeo – Volume 10' in a Service Station somewhere off the M4) Kevin ends up back at Emily's flat, somewhere near Battersea. She invites him to check out her music collection and put something on as she makes coffee. It's all mind numbingly bland 'laid back soul' and not particularly diverse either. She returns with coffee. He shows her the CD he has selected, and she nods approvingly , thinking he's impressed by her taste in music.

The bongos and sax solo starts up and her eyes roll, as this is 'one of her favourite songs ever.'

Kevin turns the volume down slightly so that it's still audible, but not obtrusive to any conversation.......

What's goin' on

He was in the box
commentating for Radio 4
on England Vs India at the Oval.

That's when I last
saw Marvin Gaye, yet

for a man
with well-documented troubles

to me, at least,
he seemed genuinely at peace

amongst his fellow
public school homosexual
opportunists

the sort who lure
Vietnamese teenage boys
into their dusty leather studies

make them recite
Blake, verbatim, in Latin.

Who knows
what History makes
of the assassination of idols
other than false mythology, but

during tiffin
Jaffers, Jeffers and 'other-handed Crispin'

popping out for a cream cake and TS Eliot break
had left Marvin in charge.

The moment was stolen
as the penny ceased to spin
by Marvin's cross-dressing Dad.

Gun put to his head,
trigger pulled,
soul splattered
all over the walls

From Exit wounds
gushed pointless platitudes
to be bled by those

who had long since forgotten
what it was they'd been slaves to.

Allegedly the only witness
was a man in shades,
his head swaying from side to side.

He claims he saw nothing,
I have my doubts.

Kevin then finishes his coffee, takes a moment to observe the look on Emily's face
and then asks if she has a number for a minicab.

It's Sunday evening. Kevin is in his living room trying not to think about the impending working week ahead but to no avail.

The room is minimal (wooden floor, white walls and a chocolate leather sofa).

On the wall is a poster of Jarvis Cocker, who like the Mona Lisa, looks like he's pointing at you with his middle finger wherever you are in the room.

Kevin switches the TV on and after channel hopping stops to watch a documentary.
During the break, he gets up, wanders aimlessly, heads towards the toilet.

He stops, decides he doesn't want to go and heads over to a door in the corner of the room.

It is not known what is behind the door or where it leads to.

Kevin turns the handle and opens the door
which then leads into the following poem.......

There's a young girl I keep in a cupboard for special occasions

though there was nothing particularly significant about that Sunday evening when I took her out towards the end of an ad break.

Who's that?	It's David Shrigley
Who's he?	He's an artist
What's an artist?	It's somebody who does art.
What is art?	Well art..... is kinda like a circus that doesn't use any animals
What's a circus?	A circus is sort of an attempt to combine zoos and cabaret
A ZOO?	Is where people go to look at animals
	AND... a cabaret is a big show with lots of colours
So... Is art a big show with lots of colours where people go to see animals that are not there?	
	Get back in your cupboard. I can do with some time to myself.

The girl walks back to the door she earlier emerged from and shuts it behind her.
Kevin follows her and locks it. At this point the phone rings. He giggles, wondering if whoever is on the other end heard his plea for time to himself and is
deliberately calling him. After all, it's what he'd do. The momentary joviality subsides into annoyance that it won't stop ringing. Resigned, Kevin walks over and picks it up....

Absolute zero

Since giving up drinking
my nights have been soaked
in conceits, deceit;

hangovers
replaced by getting over
one night stands after
jumping into bed
with the first passing bad dream

which, even though I called a cab,
left with my feet - I saw them poking
out the top of its
floral print bag,
now I don't know where I stand,
left with this, lips welded together
by an ice lolly kiss.

Yes;
I should've been careful
what I wished for

but she was nothing like
that mountain bike

promised that night by stars
that winked at a sniggering moon.

Soon;
doctor's due to call me
with the results from my tests

take my mind off this and
related anxieties by
wallpapering the flat
with women's magazines
till I'm dizzy on

a hundred and fifty fashion ideas
found by men;
mascara tips from inside
the Klu Klux Klan;

'Dear Irma, how do I tell him
it's me,
not him
when I haven't even met him and
it's actually him?'

David Bowie cover band seeks
David Bowie (or nearest offer)

cos the perfect skin you now enjoy
once chained itself to railings,

'if I knew how I felt myself
I'd probably ask him the same question'.

With what little time I have left
I manage to slip in a tarot;
quick, discreet visit
to those glamour girls of Narnia;

upturning cards all of which are
the uncertain smiles of conduits
death, the hanging man
'Look, this isn't as bad as it seems.'

Phone rings.

'Congratulations, Mr Reinhardt
you did nothing wrong in your sleep.

As for that chill you felt
when you woke
the correct medical term for it is
'Absolute Zero'.

Anyway enough about me.

How've you been Mum?
How are Dad and the cats
getting along?

Monday morning 9:32am

Kevin walks into the doctors' surgery waiting room, goes straight to the receptionist, hands his appointment card over. He keeps looking at her, he's not sure what it is, but he can't stop. She is aware of this and doesn't make eye contact.

He takes a seat. Taking a piece of paper out of his pocket he surveys the surroundings and checks items off his list:

Woman with arm in sling – Tick

Child with head in saucepan – Tick

Man sitting with a self assured posture, gel-stiffened
Mohawk, watch and mobile phone to match,
with a furrowed brow and uncharacteristic not-so-self-
assured look – Tick

Little girl with a kitten wrapped in a blanket on her lap,
wondering if she's in the right place,
constantly looking over to her Mum, who's reading the
horoscopes from an out of date woman's magazine – Tick

Kevin looks across the waiting room back at the blonde
receptionist who finally makes eye contact with him. It is
then Kevin realises what it is about her that is so compelling.
That's it, yes,
she has a beard.
He starts to shiver and convulse.
Gazing back at him and only him, she breaks into song....

Susans

I got the susans,
yeah,
I got the susans
man,
I got the susans.

Susan one:
scratched her name
on my lighter
in invisible ink

That night of spies
Disney wept and cried -
'it's all been one big fucking lie'-
oblivious

to cracked madonnas
walking their porcelain dogs
which barked glue
and made it better.

Susan two:
would dance like a fruit machine
paying out, round a handbag
which held as many
dead mice as it did diamonds.

Sent me her muff through the post.
Shrunk sucked pink gobstopper eyes
would stare at me, from next to the E45
itch-relief cream
on the mantelpiece
just below
the portrait of Mother.

Susan three:
The book I would get round to reading
if only I could get
the voice of the talking one
out of my head.

Mental note:
must get round to it
before she goes out of print.

Susan four:
I had a cowboy in Sweden's
chance at this
cultural exchange with God
like no other.
Abject acts of devotion included
abstinence from meat, masturbation
and the ultimate in self debasement:

Pot Noodle breakfast
during a Hollyoaks omnibus

Susan five:
With a name like that
a first love naturally chose itself
from the available pool of girls
who wore braces on their teeth.

Suzanne:
Between her lollipop hands and
my salivating palms
we were inseparable

thought I didn't do it with her
till he became her ex
that first and fatal night
which ended in

hospitalisation and some
excuse of a kidney infection.

To this day
she refuses to concede
that it could've been
oh so different

had she had let me
go down on her.

Still a bit sticky from that one.

I got the susans,
yeah,
I got the susans
man,
I got those susans.

Mr Reinhardt, the doctor will see you

now.

my love shines on
my love shines on
my love shines on

'Movin' on up' Primal Scream